A 3-minute forever book

EAT YOUR PEAS®

for Sons

By Cheryl Karpen
Gently Spoken

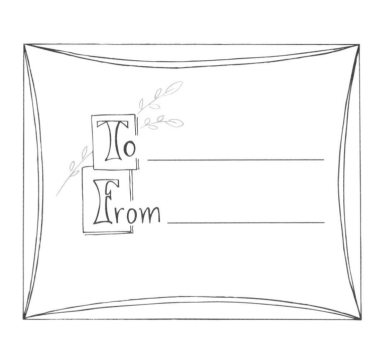

To _____

From _____

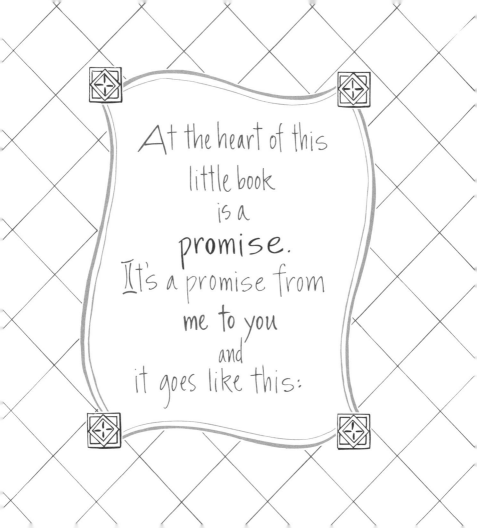

At the heart of this
little book
is a
promise.
It's a promise from
me to you
and
it goes like this:

If you ever need someone to **talk** to
(really talk to),
someone who will **listen**
(really listen),
To your **dreams**,
your **joys**,
or your **worries**,
I promise I will be there for you
day or night
through good times and tough times.

In the meantime, there are
some things I'd like you to know:

like how important you are to me,
how I only want the best for you,
and how I wish you
great happiness in life.

I am so blessed.
You
are my son.

When you were
first placed in my arms,
I had no idea
what wonders awaited me.

Just think...

I was remembering things about you
before you were able
to remember things for yourself.

(Anything you'd like to know?)

I can't help
but
Smile
every time
I
think of
the person
you've
become.

I wish for you
the very best kind of success:

Doing what you love to do.

Serving others.

Peace of mind.

Loving others and yourself.

Making a difference.

You
can do
anything
you set your mind to ...

You are capable of doing
remarkable things.

You are
intelligent,
strong,
and
competent.

Remind yourself often.

Keep a **dream**
in your pocket
and
faith in your heart.

Anything is possible!

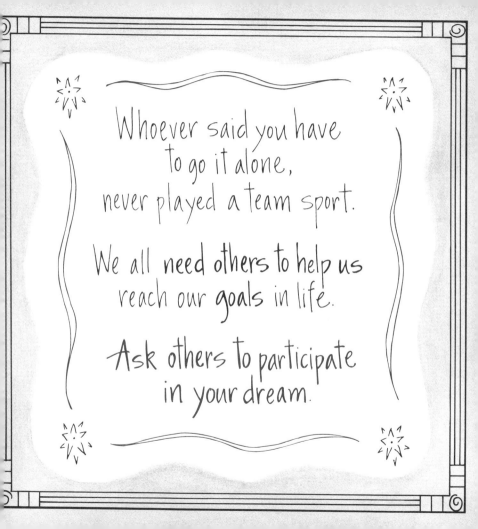

Whoever said you have
to go it alone,
never played a team sport.

We all need others to help us
reach our goals in life.

Ask others to participate
in your dream.

Life is filled with choices.

Choose carefully.

Always **reach** for,
wait for,
work for,
what will make you
feel alive
and
complete in life.

WORK HARD
but remember
to
take time to play.

Open yourself
to
love
and
being loved.
You'll never forget the feeling.

Sometimes it isn't easy being a man.
The world asks you to be
strong and courageous
when you may not
always feel that
way.

It's okay to
express feelings
and emotion.
Even tears.

May you come to recognize them
as part of life and healing.

Even in the
deepest heartache
there is grace in **humor.**

May we always know
how to **make each other smile**
and give each other reason to
hope.

There is no challenge in life so big we can't handle it together.

Remember my *promise*...

I will always be there for you.

I will always be the one
cheering the loudest
for you...

Whether on the sidelines or in my heart.

I love you
with all my
heart and soul.

I know that in our lives together
I have said and done
things I would take back
if I could.

I would never intentionally
hurt you and am sorry
when I have.

You are so very precious to me.

We all make mistakes in life.

No one is perfect.

Not even those who
love you most.

There will be
times in our life
when we simply will
not agree or understand
one another.

And that's okay.

One day we may even
laugh about it.

My dream for you

is for you to live your own dream.

Wherever you go
and
wherever I am,
there will always be a

welcome home
for you
in my heart.

Think big.

Travel light.

Seek knowledge.

Be kind.

Be really kind.

Laugh often.

Forgive others.

Forgive yourself.

Live intentionally.

Live the life you dream of...
(Go for it!)

Embrace your gifts and talents...
(You have so very many!)

Be all you can be...
(Your future looks as bright as you are!)

And most of all, **stay healthy**...
Remember to always

Eat Your Peas!

Why Peas?

She was a vibrant, dazzling young woman with a promising future.
Yet, at sixteen, her world felt sad and hopeless.

I was living over 1800 miles away and wanted to let this very special young person in my life know I would be there for her across the miles and through the darkness. I wanted her to know she could call me any time, at any hour, and I would be there for her. And I wanted to give her a piece of my heart she could take with her anywhere—a reminder she was loved.
Really loved.

Her name is Maddy and she was the inspiration for my first PEAS book, Eat Your Peas for Young Adults. At the very beginning of her book I made a place to write in my phone number so she knew I was serious about being available. And right beside the phone number I put my promise to listen—really listen—whenever that call came.

Soon after the book was published, people began to ask me if I had the same promise and affirmation for adults. I realized it isn't just young people who need to be reminded how truly special they are. We all do.

Today Maddy is thriving and giving hope to others in her life.
If someone has given you this book it means you are a pretty amazing person to them and they wanted to let you know. Take it to heart.

Believe it, and remind yourself often.

Wishing you peas and plenty of joy,

Cheryl Karpen

P.S. My mama always said, "Eat Your Peas! They're good for you."
The pages of this book are filled with nutrients for your heart.
They're simply good for you, too!

A note from the author

When you invite others to participate in
your dream, amazing things really do begin to happen.

Eat Your Peas for Sons is the seventh book
in the Eat Your Peas Collection. Its creation would not
be possible without the loving artistry of illustrator,
Sandy Fougner and editor, Suzanne Foust.
Thank you, Sandy and Suzanne, for so generously
sharing your amazing gifts and talents.

If this book has touched your life or the life of someone
you have given an Eat Your Peas book to, we'd love to hear your
story. Please send it to mystory@eatyourpeas.com

— Cheryl Karpen

A portion of the profits from the Eat Your Peas Collection will
benefit empowerment programs for youth and adults.

Other books by Cheryl Karpen

The Eat Your Peas Collection™

is now available in the following titles:

Daughters
Mothers
Sisters
Grandkids
Daughter-in-law
Girlfriends

Tough Times
Someone Special
Birthdays
New Moms
Extraordinary
   Young Person

New titles are SPROUTING up all the time!

Heart and Soul Collection

To Let You Know I Care
Hope for a Hurting Heart
Can We Try Again? Finding a way back to love

For more inspiration, Like us on Facebook at the Eat Your Peas Collection.
For quotes and pretties to post, follow us on Pinterest at
www.pinterest.com/eatyourpeasbook/

To view a complete collection of our products, visit us online at www.eatyourpeas.com

Eat Your Peas® for Sons

Home grown in the USA

For more information or to locate a store near you, contact:
Gently Spoken
PO Box 245
Anoka, MN 55303

Toll-free 1-877-224-7886 or visit us online at
www.eatyourpeas.com

 30% post-consumer recycled paper